1

Hassan Najmy
Eberstaedter Strasse 24-26
64367 Muehltal
Germany
hassannajmy1@gmail.com

Author's Note

I've lived with cats before, but it wasn't until my wife brought home two that I realised just how little I knew about these enigmatic creatures. One cat, in particular, seemed to have instantly disliked me. While my wife basked in the warmth of a purring lap cat, I found myself on the receiving end of aloofness and avoidance. Determined to bridge this feline divide, I embarked on a quest to understand the intricacies of cat behaviour. This book is a result of that journey. I hope that by sharing my discoveries, I can help other cat owners build stronger bonds with their furry companions, even the most elusive ones.

Cover photo credits: Ulrike Prisching

Dedication

To **Ulrike**, my beloved wife,

This book is dedicated to your unwavering love for our feline companions.

It all began with the arrival of our dear brother-and-sister duo. You cherished them with an open heart, giving them a warm and loving home. While the loss of our big, adventurous boy brought you sadness and sorrow, you channelled your grief into loving his little sister even more. Your strength and compassion have been truly inspiring.

Thank you for nurturing the idea of this book and encouraging me to embark on this journey of exploring the world of cats. Your passion for these creatures and your unwavering support have been the driving force behind every page.

This book is as much a tribute to your love for cats as it is a guide for others. May it bring joy and understanding to all who read it, just as you have brought joy and experience into our lives.

With all my love,

Hassan Najmy

Purr-fect Companion: A Guide to Living with Your Feline Friend

Bringing Home Your New Furry Housemate

Chapter 1

Welcoming a cat into your home is a joyous and rewarding experience. Still, it comes with a responsibility to ensure that both you and your new feline companion are comfortable and happy. The first chapter of your journey with a cat involves three crucial steps: **preparing your home for a cat, choosing the right cat for your lifestyle,** and **introducing your cat to their new environment**. Each of these steps plays a vital role in creating a harmonious relationship between you and your furry housemate.

Preparing Your Home for a Cat

Before your new cat steps paw into your home, it's essential to make sure that the environment is welcoming, safe, and stimulating. Preparing your home involves a combination of setting up a comfortable living space, securing potentially dangerous areas, and ensuring you have all the necessary supplies.

1. **Set Up a Cozy Living Space**

   Cats are territorial animals that value their personal space. Creating a cozy and inviting area for your cat can help them feel at ease. Start by designating a quiet corner of your home where your cat can retreat. This can be a small room or a dedicated area equipped with a comfortable bed, blankct, and some toys. Ensure the area is free from loud noises and heavy foot traffic, allowing your cat to relax and adjust to their new surroundings.

2.

3. **Provide the Essentials**

   Equip your home with all the necessary items your cat will need. Here are some must-haves:

   - **Litter Box:** Choose a suitable litter box and place it in a quiet, accessible location. It's advisable to have one more litter box than the number of cats you have, especially in a multi-level home. Make sure to regularly clean and maintain the litter box to prevent odours and ensure hygiene.

   - **Food and Water Bowls:** Invest in sturdy bowls for food and water. Cats are creatures of habit, so try to keep their feeding area consistent and away from their litter box. Consider a water fountain, as many cats prefer running water to still water.

- **Cat Bed:** Cats love to nap, so provide a comfortable bed where they can curl up and rest. A soft blanket or a specially designed cat bed will offer them the comfort they need.
- **Scratching Posts:** Cats have a natural instinct to scratch to keep their claws healthy and mark their territory. Providing scratching posts or boards will save your furniture and help your cat exercise this instinct.
- **Toys:** Engage your cat with a variety of toys to keep them entertained and stimulated. From interactive toys like feather wands to puzzle toys, having a mix will cater to your cat's play preferences.

3. **Cat-Proof Your Home**

Cats are curious by nature, and their curiosity often leads them into potentially dangerous situations. Cat-proofing your home is essential to prevent accidents:

4.

- **Secure Cords and Wires:** Electrical cords can be enticing to cats. Secure them to prevent chewing, which can cause injury or electrical hazards. Consider using cord protectors or concealing wires behind furniture.
- **Eliminate Toxic Plants:** Some common houseplants are toxic to cats. Research and remove any plants that might pose a danger to your cat's health. Popular plants like lilies,

poinsettias, and philodendrons can be harmful if ingested.

- o **Store Chemicals and Medications Safely:** Keep household cleaning supplies, medications, and other chemicals out of your cat's reach. Use childproof locks on cabinets or store items in high locations.
- o **Secure Windows and Balconies:** Cats love to perch on windowsills and explore balconies. Install screens on windows and ensure balconies are secure to prevent accidental falls.
- o **Hide Small Objects:** Cats love to bat around small objects, but these can pose a choking hazard. Keep small items like rubber bands, paper clips, and jewellery out of your cat's reach.

4. **Create Vertical Spaces**

Cats are natural climbers and love exploring vertical spaces. Consider adding shelves, cat trees, or window perches to give your cat more opportunities for exercise and observation. These elevated areas can also provide a sense of security and comfort.

Choosing the Right Cat for Your Lifestyle

Selecting the right cat for your lifestyle is an important decision that can greatly influence your experience as a cat owner. Cats have diverse personalities and needs, and matching these with your living situation and personal preferences will ensure a harmonious relationship.

1. **Consider Your Living Environment**
2.

- ○ **Apartment or House:** If you live in a small apartment, you might want to consider a cat breed or individual cat known for being low-energy and adaptable to smaller spaces. In contrast, larger homes may be suitable for active breeds that require more room to roam.
- ○ **Outdoor Access:** Some cats thrive with outdoor access, while others are content being indoor companions. Consider whether you can provide safe outdoor experiences, such as a secure garden or a catio (a cat patio).
- ○

2. **Evaluate Your Lifestyle**

- ○ **Work Schedule:** If you work long hours, a more independent cat may be suitable, as they can entertain themselves during the day. However, if you spend a lot of time at home, you might enjoy the company of a more social and interactive cat.
- ○ **Family and Other Pets:** If you have children or other pets, consider a cat known for being sociable and tolerant. It's important to introduce cats to other household members gradually to ensure compatibility.

- ○ **Research Cat Breeds and Personalities**

- o **Breed Traits:** While each cat has a unique personality, certain breeds tend to have specific traits. For example, Siamese cats are known for being vocal and social, while Persian cats are typically laid-back and affectionate. Research breeds that align with your preferences.

- o **Adoption Options:** Consider adopting from a shelter or rescue organisation. Many wonderful cats of all ages and backgrounds are in need of loving homes. Shelter staff can often provide insight into a cat's personality, helping you find a good match.

4. **Health and Special Needs**
   - o **Medical Conditions:** Be aware that some breeds are prone to specific health issues. Regular veterinary check-ups and preventive care are essential for keeping your cat healthy.
   - o **Special Needs Cats:** Some cats have special needs due to disabilities or medical conditions. While they may require extra care, they can be incredibly rewarding companions for those willing to provide the attention they need.

5. **Age Considerations**
   - o **Kittens:** Kittens are playful and full of energy, requiring more time and effort in training and socialisation. They're ideal for owners looking

for an interactive experience and who have the time to dedicate to raising a young cat.

- **Adult Cats:** Adult cats are often more settled and predictable in their behaviour. They might be better suited for those who prefer a companion with an established personality.
- **Senior Cats:** Senior cats are often overlooked in shelters, but they can make wonderful companions. They tend to be calmer and may require less active playtime. Adopting a senior cat can be a fulfilling experience, providing them with a loving home in their golden years.

Introducing Your Cat to Their New Environment

Once you've chosen your new feline friend, the next step is to introduce them to their new environment. This process requires patience and understanding, as cats can be sensitive to changes in their surroundings. A gradual and gentle introduction will help your cat feel safe and secure.

1. **Start Slowly**
   - **Isolation Room:** Initially, confine your cat to a single room with all their essentials—food, water, litter box, bed, and toys. This smaller space allows them to acclimate to their new surroundings without feeling overwhelmed.
   - **Gradual Exploration:** Once your cat seems comfortable in their isolation room, allow them to explore other areas of your home gradually.

Open doors to new rooms one at a time, giving your cat the freedom to explore at their own pace.

2. **Establish Routines**
   - **Consistent Feeding Times:** Cats thrive on routine. Establish regular feeding times to provide structure and stability in their daily life. Consistent feeding schedules help build trust between you and your cat.

   - **Playtime and Interaction:** Spend quality time interacting with your cat through play and gentle petting. Use toys that mimic prey-like movements, such as feather wands or laser pointers, to engage your cat's natural hunting instincts.

3. **Introduce Family Members and Other Pets**
   - **Meeting Humans:** Gradually introduce your cat to other family members, especially children. Teach children how to approach and handle cats gently, respecting their boundaries.

   - **Meeting Other Pets:** If you have other pets, introduce them to your new cat slowly and under controlled conditions. Allow them to sniff each other through a barrier, such as a baby gate, before allowing face-to-face interactions.

4. **Monitor Behaviour and Health**
   - **Observe Behaviour:** Keep an eye on your cat's behaviour for signs of stress or discomfort. Common signs include hiding, excessive grooming, or aggression. If your cat exhibits these behaviours, give them space and time to adjust.

   - **Schedule a Vet Visit:** Within the first few weeks of bringing your cat home, schedule a veterinary check-up to ensure they are healthy and up-to-date on vaccinations. This visit also allows you to discuss any concerns or questions you may have with a professional.

5. **Create a Safe Haven**
   - **Hiding Spots:** Provide hiding spots throughout your home where your cat can retreat when they feel anxious or need some alone time. This can be a cosy box, a covered bed, or even a quiet corner.

   - **Calming Aids:** Consider using pheromone diffusers or sprays designed to reduce stress and promote a sense of calm in cats. These products can be particularly helpful during the initial adjustment period.

6. Patience is Key

- o **Respect Their Space:** Allow your cat to come to you on their terms. Avoid forcing interactions or overwhelming them with attention. Let them decide when they are ready for affection and exploration.

- o **Celebrate Small Victories:** Each small step your cat takes towards becoming comfortable in their new home is a victory. Celebrate these moments and acknowledge your cat's progress with gentle encouragement.

Conclusion

Bringing a new cat into your home is a joyful experience that requires thoughtful preparation and consideration. By preparing your home, choosing the right cat for your lifestyle, and introducing them to their new environment with care and patience, you lay the foundation for a lasting and loving relationship with your furry housemate. Remember, every cat is unique, and understanding their individual needs and preferences will ensure a happy and harmonious coexistence.

Chapter 2

Feeding Your Feline Friend

Feeding your feline friend is more than just a routine task—it's a vital part of ensuring your cat's health, happiness, and longevity. A well-nourished cat is not only healthier but also more energetic, playful, and content. In this chapter, we'll explore three critical aspects of cat feeding: **selecting the right cat food, establishing feeding schedules and portion sizes,** and **dealing with picky eaters and dietary needs**. Understanding these facets will help you make informed decisions about your cat's diet, contributing to their overall well-being.

Selecting the Right Cat Food

Choosing the right cat food is the foundation of your pet's nutrition. With a wide variety of options available on the market, selecting the right diet for your cat can be overwhelming. It's essential to understand the nutritional needs of your cat and how different types of cat food meet these requirements.

Understanding Nutritional Needs

Cats are obligate carnivores, which means they require a diet rich in animal proteins and fats to thrive. Their bodies are uniquely adapted to digest and utilise nutrients from meat, and they have specific dietary requirements that must be met:

1. **Protein:** Proteins are crucial for building and repairing tissues, producing enzymes and hormones, and supporting overall bodily functions. High-quality animal-based proteins, such as chicken, beef, or fish, are essential for your cat's diet.

2. **Taurine:** Taurine is an amino acid vital for maintaining heart health, vision, and reproduction in cats. Unlike some animals, cats cannot synthesise taurine on their own and must obtain it from their diet. Ensure that the cat food you choose contains sufficient taurine levels.

3. **Fats:** Fats are a primary energy source for cats and are important for absorbing fat-soluble vitamins (A, D, E, and K). Omega-3 and Omega-6 fatty acids, found in fish oils and animal fats, contribute to healthy skin and a shiny coat.

4. **Vitamins and Minerals:** Vitamins and minerals play a crucial role in various bodily functions, including immune support and bone health. Look for cat foods fortified with essential vitamins and minerals like calcium, phosphorus, and vitamin E.

5. **Water:** Cats have a low thirst drive compared to other animals and may not drink enough water on their own. Therefore, wet cat food can be a good option to ensure your cat stays hydrated.

Types of Cat Food

The market offers a wide range of cat food types, each with its own benefits and drawbacks. Understanding these options can help you choose the best food for your cat's specific needs:

1. **Dry Cat Food (Kibble):**

   - **Pros:** Dry cat food is convenient, easy to store, and has a long shelf life. It's generally more cost-effective and can help maintain dental health by reducing tartar buildup.

   - **Cons:** Kibble typically contains less moisture than wet food, which may lead to dehydration in some cats. Additionally, some brands may contain fillers and carbohydrates that are less suitable for a cat's diet.

2. **Wet Cat Food (Canned):**

   - **Pros:** Wet cat food is rich in moisture, helping keep your cat hydrated. It often contains fewer carbohydrates and more protein, making it a closer match to a cat's natural diet.

   - **Cons:** Wet food can be more expensive and less convenient to store once opened. It also has a shorter shelf life than dry food.

3. **Semi-Moist Cat Food:**

   - **Pros:** Semi-moist foods offer a middle ground between dry and wet food, providing more moisture than kibble but with more convenience than canned food.

   - **Cons:** This type of food often contains more artificial additives and preservatives, which might not be ideal for all cats.

4. **Raw and Homemade Diets:**

   - **Pros:** A raw diet aims to mimic what a cat would naturally eat in the wild. It's high in protein and moisture, with no artificial additives.

   - **Cons:** Preparing a raw diet at home requires careful planning to ensure nutritional balance and to avoid the risk of bacterial contamination. It can also be time-consuming and more costly.

5. **Grain-Free and Specialty Diets:**

   - **Pros:** These diets are formulated for cats with specific dietary needs or allergies, offering specialised nutrition.

   - **Cons:** Grain-free diets aren't necessary for all cats and can sometimes be more expensive without providing significant health benefits for every feline.

How to Choose the Best Cat Food

When selecting cat food, consider the following factors to ensure you're making the best choice for your pet:

1. **Life Stage:** Choose a formula appropriate for your cat's life stage—kitten, adult, or senior. Kittens require more protein and calories for growth, while seniors may benefit from joint-supporting nutrients and fewer calories.

2. **Health Conditions:** If your cat has specific health issues, such as urinary tract problems or food allergies, consult your veterinarian for dietary recommendations.

3. **Brand Reputation:** Opt for brands known for quality and transparency in their ingredient sourcing and manufacturing processes. Check for recalls or complaints about the brand to ensure safety.

4. **Ingredient List:** Look for cat foods with high-quality animal proteins listed as the first ingredient. Avoid foods with excessive fillers, artificial colours, and by-products.

5. **Palatability:** Cats have individual tastes, so finding a food that your cat enjoys eating is essential for maintaining their health and happiness.

Feeding Schedules and Portion Sizes

Establishing a consistent feeding schedule and determining the correct portion sizes are key to maintaining your cat's ideal weight and overall health. Unlike dogs, cats are natural grazers, often preferring to eat several small meals throughout the day.

Feeding Schedules

Here are a few feeding schedule options that cater to different lifestyles and cat preferences:

1. **Free Feeding:** Allow your cat to have constant access to food, letting them eat whenever they desire.

   - **Pros:** This method is convenient for busy owners and suits cats who can self-regulate their food intake without overeating.

   - **Cons:** Free feeding can lead to overeating and weight gain in cats who don't control their portions well. It's not ideal for multi-cat households where one cat may dominate the food source.

2. **Scheduled Feeding:** Offer meals at specific times of the day, typically two to three times daily.

   - **Pros:** Scheduled feeding helps control portion sizes and monitor your cat's appetite, making it easier to notice any changes in eating habits that might indicate health issues.

   - **Cons:** This method requires more time and attention from the owner, which might not be suitable for those with hectic schedules.

3. **Combination Feeding:** Provide dry food for free feeding and supplement with scheduled wet food meals.

   - **Pros:** This approach offers the benefits of both free feeding and scheduled feeding, allowing your cat to graze on dry food while receiving the hydration and nutritional benefits of wet food.

   - **Cons:** Combination feeding may still lead to weight gain if portion sizes are not carefully controlled.

Determining Portion Sizes

Proper portion control is crucial for preventing obesity and ensuring your cat receives the nutrients they need without overfeeding. Consider the following guidelines when determining portion sizes:

1. **Read the Feeding Guidelines:** Most commercial cat foods provide feeding guidelines on the packaging based on your cat's weight and age. Use these recommendations as a starting point and adjust based on your cat's activity level and individual needs.

2. **Monitor Weight and Condition:** Regularly check your cat's weight and body condition. A healthy cat should have a

visible waistline and ribs that can be felt but not seen. Adjust portion sizes if your cat is gaining or losing weight.

3. **Consider Activity Level:** Active cats, such as those who frequently play or spend time outdoors, may require more calories than sedentary indoor cats.

4. **Consult Your Veterinarian:** If you're unsure about the appropriate portion size for your cat, consult your veterinarian. They can provide personalised advice based on your cat's health, age, and activity level.

Dealing with Picky Eaters and Dietary Needs

Some cats can be notoriously picky eaters, turning up their noses at certain foods or flavours. Additionally, specific dietary needs may require adjustments to your cat's feeding regimen. Here are some strategies to address these challenges:

Dealing with Picky Eaters

1. **Try Different Flavours and Textures:** Cats have individual preferences when it comes to flavours and textures. Experiment with various options to find what your cat enjoys. Some cats prefer pate over chunks, while others might favour fish over poultry flavours.

2. **Gradual Transition:** If you're switching your cat's food, do it gradually by mixing the new food with the old food over

a week. This gradual transition can help avoid digestive upset and increase acceptance of the new diet.

3. **Enhance Palatability:** Add a bit of warm water or low-sodium chicken broth to your cat's food to enhance its aroma and flavour. Some cats find warm food more appealing, as it mimics the temperature of freshly caught prey.

4. **Limit Treats:** Excessive treats can spoil your cat's appetite for their regular meals. Limit treats to no more than 10% of your cat's daily caloric intake and use them as rewards for positive behaviour rather than frequent snacks.

5. **Establish a Routine:** Cats appreciate routine, and feeding them at the same times each day can create a sense of anticipation and consistency, making them more likely to eat their meals.

6. **Consult a Vet:** If your cat's picky eating persists and results in weight loss or malnutrition, consult your veterinarian to rule out underlying health issues such as dental problems or gastrointestinal disorders.

Addressing Dietary Needs

1. **Weight Management:** If your cat is overweight, consider switching to a weight management formula designed to reduce calorie intake while providing essential nutrients. Encourage regular

exercise through play to help your cat maintain a healthy weight.

2. **Allergies and Sensitivities:** Some cats may develop allergies or sensitivities to specific ingredients, resulting in digestive issues or skin problems. If you suspect your cat has a food allergy, consult your veterinarian for advice on hypoallergenic diets or elimination trials.

3. **Special Diets for Health Conditions:** Cats with certain health conditions, such as diabetes or kidney disease, may require specialised diets tailored to their needs. These diets often contain controlled levels of protein, phosphorus, or carbohydrates and should be administered under the guidance of a veterinarian.

4. **Senior Cats:** As cats age, their nutritional requirements change. Senior cat food formulas often include added joint-supporting nutrients and lower calorie content to suit their changing metabolism. Ensure your senior cat receives appropriate nutrition to support their health and longevity.

Conclusion

Feeding your feline friend is an essential aspect of responsible pet ownership that requires careful consideration of their nutritional needs, feeding schedules, and portion sizes. By selecting the right cat food, establishing a consistent feeding routine, and addressing any picky eating behaviours or dietary requirements, you can ensure your cat enjoys a healthy, balanced diet that supports their overall well-being. Remember, each cat is unique, and understanding their individual preferences and needs will help you provide the best possible care for your beloved companion.

Chapter 3:

Keeping Your Cat Healthy and Happy

Ensuring that your cat leads a healthy and happy life involves more than just providing food and shelter. It requires a holistic approach that encompasses regular veterinary care, proper grooming, and providing both mental and physical stimulation. This chapter will delve into these essential aspects of cat care, helping you lay the groundwork for a long, joyful life with your feline companion.

Establishing a Veterinary Routine

One of the most crucial steps in keeping your cat healthy is establishing a consistent veterinary routine. Regular veterinary visits play a pivotal role in preventing and managing health issues, ensuring your cat lives a long and comfortable life.

Importance of Regular Vet Visits

- **Early Detection of Health Issues:** Routine check-ups allow your veterinarian to detect potential health problems early, before they develop into serious issues. Early diagnosis often leads to more effective treatment and a better prognosis.

- **Vaccinations:** Cats require vaccinations to protect them against common diseases such as feline distemper, rabies, and feline leukaemia. Your veterinarian will establish a vaccination schedule based on your cat's age, lifestyle, and health status.

- **Parasite Prevention:** Fleas, ticks, and worms are common parasites that can affect your cat's health. Regular vet visits ensure your cat is protected through preventive measures, such as topical treatments or oral medications.

- **Weight Management:** Obesity is a prevalent issue among cats, leading to various health problems. Regular vet visits include weight checks, and your vet can offer guidance on maintaining your cat's ideal weight through diet and exercise.

- **Dental Health:** Dental issues, like gum disease and tooth decay, can affect your cat's overall health. Your veterinarian will check your cat's teeth and gums during visits and may recommend dental cleanings to prevent oral health problems.

Creating a Veterinary Schedule

1. **Kittens (Up to 1 Year):** Kittens require frequent vet visits, typically every 3-4 weeks until they are about 16 weeks old. During these visits, they will receive vaccinations, deworming, and a general health assessment. Discuss spaying or neutering with your vet around 4-6 months of age.

2. **Adult Cats (1-7 Years):** For healthy adult cats, annual check-ups are generally sufficient. These visits include vaccinations, parasite prevention, dental checks, and a physical examination to ensure your cat remains healthy.

3. **Senior Cats (7+ Years):** Senior cats should visit the vet at least twice a year. These visits often include blood work, urinalysis, and other diagnostic tests to monitor age-related health issues like kidney disease, arthritis, or diabetes.

Choosing the Right Veterinarian

- **Research and Recommendations:** Ask friends, family, or your local pet community for veterinarian recommendations. Online reviews can also provide insights into a vet's reputation and the quality of care provided.

- **Consider Location:** Choose a veterinary clinic conveniently located near your home to make appointments more accessible, especially in emergencies.

- **Evaluate the Clinic:** Visit the clinic to assess its cleanliness, organisation, and staff friendliness. A welcoming environment can make vet visits less stressful for both you and your cat.

- **Communication:** Select a vet who communicates clearly and listens to your concerns. A good vet should be willing to discuss treatment options and answer any questions you may have about your cat's health.

Grooming and Hygiene

Grooming and maintaining your cat's hygiene is essential not only for their physical appearance but also for their health and well-being. Proper grooming helps prevent matting, reduces hairballs, and keeps your cat comfortable and clean.

Regular Brushing

- **Fur Maintenance:** Regular brushing helps remove loose hair, preventing matting and reducing the occurrence of hairballs. The frequency of brushing depends on your cat's coat type—long-haired cats may require daily brushing, while short-haired breeds might only need weekly grooming.

- **Bonding Experience:** Grooming your cat is an excellent opportunity for bonding. Use a soft brush or grooming mitt to gently stroke your cat, making the experience enjoyable for both of you.

- **Deshedding Tools:** Invest in a quality de-shedding tool for long-haired cats to manage to shed and minimise tangles.

Bathing

- **When to Bathe:** Most cats are self-cleaning and rarely need baths. However, if your cat becomes particularly dirty or has a medical condition requiring bathing, use a gentle, cat-specific shampoo. Always consult your veterinarian before bathing your cat.

- **How to Bathe:** If bathing is necessary, fill a sink or tub with warm water and gently wet your cat, avoiding the head area. Apply shampoo, rinse thoroughly, and wrap your cat in a warm towel to dry. Use a hairdryer on a low setting if your cat tolerates it.

Nail Trimming

- **Why Trim Nails:** Regular nail trimming prevents overgrowth, which can lead to pain or injury. Long nails may cause difficulty walking or get snagged on surfaces, potentially leading to injuries.

- **How to Trim:** Use a cat-specific nail clipper, and gently press on the paw to extend the claw. Trim the tip, avoiding the quick (the pink part inside the nail). If you're unsure, ask your vet for a demonstration or seek professional grooming services.

Dental Care

- **Brushing Teeth:** Dental hygiene is crucial for preventing periodontal disease. Use a cat-specific toothbrush and toothpaste to clean your cat's teeth regularly. Start slowly, allowing your cat to get used to the process.

- **Dental Treats and Toys:** Consider dental treats or toys designed to help reduce tartar and plaque buildup. These can supplement regular brushing but should not replace it.

Ear and Eye Cleaning

- **Ears:** Regularly check your cat's ears for signs of dirt, wax buildup, or infection. Use a damp cotton ball or vet-recommended ear cleaner to gently clean the outer ear, avoiding the ear canal.

- **Eyes:** Wipe away any discharge around your cat's eyes with a damp cotton ball or soft cloth. If you notice persistent discharge or irritation, consult your vet.

Providing Mental and Physical Stimulation

Cats are intelligent and active creatures that require mental and physical stimulation to prevent boredom and promote overall well-being. Engaging your cat's mind and body can help reduce behavioural problems, such as excessive scratching or aggression, and improve their quality of life.

Mental Stimulation

1. **Interactive Toys:** Toys that mimic prey movements, such as feather wands, laser pointers, and motorised toys, stimulate your cat's natural hunting instincts. Rotate toys regularly to keep your cat interested.

2. **Puzzle Feeders:** Puzzle feeders challenge your cat's mind and encourage natural foraging behaviour. They also slow down eating, preventing overeating and promoting healthy digestion.

3. **Training Sessions:** Teaching your cat tricks or commands can provide mental stimulation and strengthen your bond. Use positive reinforcement with treats or affection to encourage desired behaviours.

4. **Environmental Enrichment:** Create an engaging environment by providing scratching posts, climbing trees, and cosy hiding spots. Consider adding cat shelves or window perches to give your cat a high vantage point to observe their surroundings.

5. **Interactive Playtime:** Spend time playing with your cat daily. Engage them with toys that allow you to participate, fostering a strong bond between you and your feline friend.

Physical Stimulation

1. **Play Sessions:** Schedule regular play sessions to keep your cat physically active. Engage in interactive play using toys like feather wands, balls, or laser pointers to encourage running, jumping, and pouncing.

2. **Outdoor Exploration:** If safe, supervised outdoor exploration can provide excellent physical stimulation.

Consider a secure outdoor enclosure (catio) or take your cat for walks on a harness and leash to explore the outside world safely.

3. **Climbing and Jumping Opportunities:** Cats love to climb and jump. Provide cat trees, shelves, or furniture that allow your cat to climb and explore vertical spaces. This not only promotes exercise but also gives them a sense of territory and safety.

4. **Agility Training:** Set up a mini agility course in your home with obstacles like tunnels, hoops, and ramps. Guide your cat through the course using treats and praise, providing both physical exercise and mental stimulation.

Addressing Boredom and Behavioural Issues

1. **Routine Variation:** Keep your cat engaged by varying their daily routine. Introduce new toys, rotate old ones, and offer different types of enrichment activities to prevent boredom.

2. **Avoid Overstimulation:** While stimulation is essential, avoid overwhelming your cat with too much activity or noise. Respect their need for rest and alone time, ensuring a balanced lifestyle.

3. **Addressing Behavioural Problems:** If your cat displays undesirable behaviours, such as scratching furniture or aggression, identify potential triggers and work to address

them. Boredom, stress, or health issues can contribute to behavioural problems, and a vet consultation may be necessary.

∫Some cats benefit from having another feline friend. If you're considering adopting another cat, ensure proper introductions and monitor their interactions to promote harmony.

Keeping Your Cat's Mind Sharp

1. **Senior Cats:** As cats age, their cognitive abilities may decline. Engage senior cats with gentle play and puzzles to keep their minds active. Provide comfortable resting spots and maintain a stable routine to reduce stress.

2. **Environmental Changes:** Introduce changes gradually to avoid overwhelming your cat. Cats are creatures of habit, and sudden changes can lead to stress or anxiety. Maintain familiar routines while slowly introducing new elements.

Conclusion

Keeping your cat healthy and happy involves a combination of regular veterinary care, grooming, and providing mental and physical stimulation. By establishing a veterinary routine, maintaining proper hygiene, and ensuring your cat remains engaged and active, you can significantly enhance their quality of life. Remember, each cat is unique, so understanding and catering to your feline friend's individual needs will help foster a strong, loving bond and ensure they lead a fulfilling life.

Chapter 4

Navigating the Joys and Challenges of Cat Ownership

Cats are enigmatic creatures, celebrated for their independence, unique personalities, and quirky behaviours. As a cat owner, you embark on a rewarding journey filled with both joys and challenges. Understanding your cat's behaviour and personality is key to fostering a harmonious relationship and effectively dealing with any issues that may arise. This chapter delves into the nuances of cat behaviour, common challenges you may encounter, and strategies to build a strong bond with your feline friend.

Understanding Your Cat's Behaviour and Personality

Each cat is unique, with its distinct personality and behavioural traits. Understanding these behaviours can help you decode your cat's needs, preferences, and emotional state. Recognising the diversity in feline personalities and the various factors influencing their behaviour is crucial to providing the best care.

The Basics of Feline Behaviour

Cats are often misunderstood due to their complex behaviours, which can sometimes appear aloof or mysterious. However, understanding the fundamentals of feline behaviour can help demystify your cat's actions and improve your relationship with them. Here are some key aspects to consider:

1. **Territorial Nature:**

- **Space:** Cats are territorial animals. They often establish and defend their territory, which includes their home and any areas they frequent. This territorial behaviour explains why they might scratch furniture, mark certain spots, or feel uneasy with new changes in their environment.

- **Marking Territory:** Cats mark their territory using scent glands located on their face, paws, and tail. Rubbing against objects or scratching surfaces is a way for cats to leave their scent and claim ownership.

2. **Body Language:**

- **Tail Position:** A cat's tail is a crucial indicator of its mood. A tail held high often signals confidence and contentment, while a low or tucked tail may indicate fear or submission. A puffed-up tail usually means the cat is frightened or agitated.

- **Ears and Eyes:** Cats communicate through their ears and eyes. Forward-facing ears and dilated pupils suggest curiosity or playfulness, while flattened ears and narrowed eyes indicate irritation or aggression.

- **Whiskers:** Cats use their whiskers to detect changes in their environment. Forward-facing whiskers indicate interest or excitement, while whiskers pulled back against the face may signal fear or discomfort.

3. **Vocalisations:**

   - **Meowing:** Cats meow primarily to communicate with humans. Different tones and pitches convey various messages, from a simple greeting to a request for food or attention.

   - **Purring:** Purring typically signifies contentment, but it can also indicate discomfort or self-soothing when a cat is stressed or unwell.

   - **Hissing and Growling:** These sounds are clear indicators of fear, aggression, or distress. It's essential to respect your cat's space when they display these vocalisations.

4. **Social Structure:**

   - **Solitary Hunters:** Cats are solitary hunters by nature. Unlike dogs, who thrive in packs, cats often prefer solitude or small, familiar groups. This independence can sometimes be misinterpreted as aloofness.

   - **Social Bonds:** Despite their independent nature, many cats form strong bonds with their human caregivers and other pets. They may seek companionship, grooming, and playtime, demonstrating affection in their unique way.

5. **Play Behaviour:**

   - **Stalking and Pouncing:** Play is an essential part of a cat's life, mimicking hunting behaviour. Cats engage in stalking, pouncing, and batting at objects to simulate catching prey, which is vital for their physical and mental well-being.

   - **Interactive Play:** Engaging in interactive play with toys that mimic prey can strengthen your bond with your cat and provide them with essential exercise and mental stimulation.

Understanding Cat Personalities

Just like humans, cats have diverse personalities, shaped by genetics, upbringing, and environmental factors. Recognising your cat's personality can help you cater to their needs and build a strong relationship. Here are some common cat personality types:

1. **The Social Butterfly:**

   - **Characteristics:** Social butterflies are friendly and outgoing, often approaching strangers and other pets with curiosity and enthusiasm. They thrive in social environments and enjoy being the centre of attention.

   - **Care Tips:** Provide ample social interaction, including playtime and petting, to keep these cats happy. They may enjoy multi-cat households or live with other pets who share their sociable nature.

2. **The Independent Explorer:**

   - **Characteristics:** Independent explorers prefer solitude and enjoy their own company. They may be wary of strangers and require time to warm up to new people or situations.

   - **Care Tips:** Respect their need for space and independence. Provide plenty of environmental enrichment, such as climbing trees or window perches, to satisfy their curiosity.

3. **The Playful Clown:**

   - **Characteristics:** Playful clowns are energetic and mischievous, often getting into everything they can find. They love interactive play and thrive on physical and mental challenges.

   - **Care Tips:** Keep these cats entertained with a variety of toys and regular play sessions. Rotate toys frequently to maintain their interest, and consider agility training or puzzle feeders to engage their minds.

4. **The Gentle Giant:**

   - **Characteristics:** Gentle giants are calm and laid-back, preferring relaxation over high-energy activities. They are typically affectionate and enjoy lounging with their favourite humans.

   - **Care Tips:** Provide comfortable resting spots and gentle affection. While they may not be as active as other personalities, ensure they receive regular play to maintain a healthy weight and stimulate their mind.

5. **The Cautious Observer:**

   - **Characteristics:** Cautious observers are shy and reserved, often taking time to assess their surroundings before engaging. They may be sensitive to changes and require a stable, predictable environment.

   - **Care Tips:** Offer a safe, quiet space for these cats to retreat when they feel overwhelmed. Introduce new experiences gradually, allowing them to explore at their own pace. Patience and gentle encouragement will help build their confidence.

The Influence of Breed and Background

While personality is often individual, certain breeds exhibit distinct traits. For example:

- **Siamese Cats:** Known for their vocal nature and sociability, Siamese cats often demand attention and enjoy being part of family activities.

- **Persian Cats:** Persian cats are typically gentle and affectionate but may be more reserved and prefer quiet environments.

- **Bengal Cats:** Bengals are highly energetic and curious, requiring ample playtime and stimulation to keep them satisfied.

Beyond breed, a cat's upbringing and background can significantly impact their behaviour and personality. Cats rescued from shelters may have unique quirks or require extra patience to overcome past traumas. Understanding your cat's history can provide insights into their behaviour and help you create a nurturing environment.

Dealing with Common Behavioural Issues

Despite our best efforts, cats can sometimes exhibit challenging behaviours that require patience and understanding. Addressing these issues involves identifying underlying causes and implementing effective strategies to encourage positive behaviour.

Common Behavioural Issues and Solutions

1. **Litter Box Problems:**

   - **Symptoms:** Cats may urinate or defecate outside the litter box, leading to frustration for both the owner and the cat.

   - **Possible Causes:** Stress, medical issues, territorial marking, or dissatisfaction with the litter box setup can contribute to litter box problems.

   - **Solutions:**

   - **Consult a Veterinarian:** Rule out medical issues, such as urinary tract infections or bladder stones, which can cause litter box avoidance.

   - **Maintain Cleanliness:** Ensure the litter box is clean and scooped daily. Cats are fastidious creatures and may avoid dirty litter boxes.

   - **Right Litter and Location:** Experiment with different types of litter and place boxes in quiet, accessible locations. Provide enough litter boxes–ideally one per cat, plus one extra.

2. **Scratching Furniture:**

   - **Symptoms:** Cats scratch furniture, carpets, or other household items, leading to damaged belongings.

- **Possible Causes:** Scratching is a natural behaviour for cats, used to mark territory, exercise, and maintain claw health.

- **Solutions:**

- **Provide Scratching Posts:** Offer a variety of scratching posts made of different materials, such as sisal, cardboard, or wood. Place them in strategic locations near where your cat likes to scratch.

Reward your cat for using scratching posts with treats or praise, encouraging them to focus on appropriate surfaces.
- **Deterrents:** Use deterrents like double-sided tape or citrus-scented sprays on furniture to discourage unwanted scratching.

3. **Aggression Towards Humans or Other Animals:**

- **Symptoms:** Cats may exhibit aggression, such as biting, hissing, or swatting, towards people or other pets.

- **Possible Causes:** Fear, stress, territorial disputes, or past trauma can lead to aggressive behaviour.

- **Solutions:**
- **Identify Triggers:** Observe what triggers your cat's aggression and try to minimise exposure to those situations.
- **Provide Safe Spaces:** Ensure your cat has access to safe spaces where they can retreat and feel secure.

- **Gradual Introductions:** When introducing new pets or people, do so gradually, allowing your cat to acclimate at their own pace.
   - **Professional Help:** If aggression persists, consult a veterinarian or a professional animal behaviourist for guidance.

4. **Separation Anxiety:**

  - **Symptoms:** Cats with separation anxiety may become distressed when left alone, displaying excessive vocalisation, destructive behaviour, or litter box issues.

  - **Possible Causes:** Attachment to their owner, changes in routine, or past abandonment experiences can contribute to separation anxiety.

 - **Solutions:**
   - **Desensitise Leaving Cues:** Gradually accustom your cat to departure cues by associating them with positive experiences

, like treats or playtime.
   - **Provide Entertainment:** Leave toys, puzzles, or interactive feeders to keep your cat engaged when you're away.
   - **Establish Routines:** Maintain consistent daily routines to provide stability and reduce anxiety.

- **Comforting Environment:** Create a comforting environment with familiar scents, cozy bedding, and background noise, such as soft music or a TV.

5. **Excessive Vocalisation:**

- **Symptoms:** Some cats may meow excessively, often seeking attention, food, or expressing discomfort.

- **Possible Causes:** Hunger, boredom, stress, medical issues, or breed tendencies can contribute to excessive vocalisation.

- **Solutions:**
  - **Rule Out Medical Issues:** Consult a veterinarian to ensure no underlying health problems are causing the behaviour.
  - **Attention and Play:** Provide ample attention, playtime, and environmental enrichment to keep your cat mentally stimulated.
  - **Scheduled Feeding:** Stick to a regular feeding schedule to prevent hunger-related vocalisation.
  - **Ignore Demand Meowing:** Avoid reinforcing demand meowing by ignoring it until your cat is calm, then reward quiet behaviour with attention or treats.

Understanding Stress and Anxiety in Cats

Stress and anxiety are common factors contributing to behavioural issues in cats. Identifying and addressing these emotions is crucial to promoting a happy, balanced life for your feline friend.

1. **Common Stress Triggers:**

- **Changes in Environment:** Moving to a new home, rearranging furniture, or introducing new pets can cause stress for cats.

- **Lack of Routine:** Cats thrive on routine, and sudden changes in their schedule can lead to anxiety.

- **Loud Noises:** Loud noises, such as thunderstorms or fireworks, can frighten and stress cats.

- **Conflict with Other Pets:** Tension between cats or other pets can lead to stress and behavioural issues.

2. **Signs of Stress:**

- **Hiding or Withdrawal:** Cats may retreat to hiding spots or become less social when stressed.

- **Excessive Grooming:** Over-grooming or self-mutilation can be a sign of stress or anxiety.

- **Aggression:** Stress may manifest as aggression towards humans or other animals.

- **Litter Box Issues:** Stress can lead to inappropriate urination or defecation outside the litter box.

3. **Managing Stress and Anxiety:**

- **Create Safe Spaces:** Provide hiding spots or cosy areas where your cat can retreat when they feel overwhelmed.

- **Feline Pheromones:** Use products like feline pheromone diffusers to create a calming environment for your cat.

- **Gradual Introductions:** Introduce new elements or changes gradually, allowing your cat to acclimate at their own pace.

- **Positive Reinforcement:** Encourage positive behaviour with treats, praise, and affection, creating a trusting and supportive environment.

- **Consult Professionals:** If stress or anxiety persists, consult a veterinarian or professional behaviourist for guidance and support.

Fostering a Strong Bond with Your Cat

Building a strong bond with your cat requires time, patience, and understanding. This bond is the foundation of a fulfilling relationship, enhancing your cat's well-being and enriching your life as a cat owner.

Steps to Strengthen Your Bond

1. **Quality Time Together:**

   - **Engage in Play:** Interactive play is an excellent way to bond with your cat. Use toys that mimic prey, like feather wands or laser pointers, to stimulate their natural hunting instincts and provide exercise.

   - **Cuddle and Relax:** Spend time cuddling or sitting with your cat, allowing them to choose when they want affection. Respect their boundaries and avoid forcing interaction.

   - **Routine Interactions:** Establish daily routines, such as feeding, grooming, or playtime, to build trust and familiarity.

2. **Positive Reinforcement:**

   - **Reward Good Behaviour:** Use treats, praise, or affection to reinforce positive behaviours, encouraging your cat to repeat them.

   - **Avoid Punishment:** Avoid using punishment or negative reinforcement, as it can damage your relationship and lead to fear or aggression.

3. **Understanding Their Needs:**

   - **Observe and Adapt:** Pay attention to your cat's preferences and adapt your interactions accordingly. Some cats may enjoy being held, while others prefer gentle petting or play.

   - **Provide Mental Stimulation:** Keep your cat mentally stimulated with toys, puzzles, and activities that challenge their mind.

   - **Respect Their Independence:** Allow your cat to have their own space and time alone. Cats value their independence and will appreciate your respect for their boundaries.

4. **Communicate Effectively:**

   - **Learn Their Language:** Understanding your cat's body language and vocalisations can help you communicate more effectively, recognising their needs and emotions.

   - **Respond to Cues:** Pay attention to your cat's cues and respond appropriately, whether they seek attention, play, or solitude.

5. **Shared Experiences:**

   - **Explore Together:** If your cat is comfortable with it, take them for walks on a leash or explore outdoor spaces safely.

Shared experiences can strengthen your bond and provide enrichment.

   - **Grooming Sessions:** Grooming can be a bonding activity, especially for long-haired breeds. Use grooming sessions as an opportunity to show care and affection.

Building Trust and Confidence

Building trust and confidence is essential for a strong, lasting bond with your cat. Trust forms the foundation of a positive relationship, allowing your cat to feel secure and valued.

1. **Consistency:**

   - **Reliable Routine:** Establish consistent routines for feeding, play, and bedtime, providing predictability and security for your cat.

   - **Consistent Behaviour:** Maintain consistent behaviour in your interactions, avoiding sudden changes that may confuse or stress your cat.

2. **Patience and Understanding:**

   - **Respect Their Pace:** Allow your cat to adjust to new situations or people at their own pace, avoiding pressure or force.

- **Be Patient:** Building trust takes time, especially for shy or previously traumatised cats. Patience and understanding are key to fostering a positive relationship.

3. **Respect Their Space:**

   - **Safe Retreats:** Provide safe retreats where your cat can escape when they feel overwhelmed or need solitude.

   - **Respect Boundaries:** Pay attention to your cat's cues and respect their boundaries, avoiding overstimulation or unwanted interactions.

Recognising the Rewards of Cat Ownership

Cat ownership comes with numerous rewards, from the joy of companionship to the satisfaction of nurturing another living being. By understanding your cat's behaviour, addressing challenges, and fostering a strong bond, you can experience the full range of benefits that come with sharing your life with a feline friend.

1. **Emotional Fulfilment:**

   - **Companionship:** Cats offer loyal companionship, providing comfort and emotional support in daily life.

   - **Affectionate Bonds:** Building a strong bond with your cat results in a rewarding, affectionate relationship that enriches your life.

2. **Mental and Physical Benefits:**

   - **Stress Relief:** Interacting with cats can reduce stress and anxiety, promoting relaxation and well-being.

   - **Physical Health:** Owning a cat has been linked to various health benefits, including lower blood pressure and reduced risk of heart disease.

3. **Entertainment and Joy:**

   - **Playful Moments:** Cats bring joy and entertainment with their playful antics and unique personalities, offering endless amusement.

   - **Shared Experiences:** Engaging in shared activities, such as play or exploration, creates cherished memories and deepens your bond.

4. **Life Lessons:**

   - **Patience and Empathy:** Caring for a cat teaches patience, empathy, and understanding, valuable skills that extend beyond pet ownership.

   - **Responsibility:** Cat ownership instils a sense of responsibility and commitment, fostering personal growth and development.

Conclusion

Navigating the joys and challenges of cat ownership involves understanding your cat's behaviour, addressing common issues, and fostering a strong bond. By recognising the uniqueness of your feline friend and investing time and effort into their care, you can create a harmonious and fulfilling relationship that benefits both you and your cat. Embrace the journey of cat ownership with patience, empathy, and a willingness to learn, and you'll find yourself rewarded with the love and companionship of a truly remarkable companion.

Chapter 5

Making the Most of Your Cat's Company

Living with a cat is a delightful experience that can enrich your life in numerous ways. Cats are known for their unique personalities, amusing quirks, and affectionate gestures. Integrating them into your daily life not only enhances your bond but also offers companionship and joy. This chapter explores how to make the most of your feline friend's company, enjoy quality time together, and appreciate the unique characteristics that make your cat truly special.

Incorporating Your Cat into Your Daily Life

Cats are more than just pets; they are companions that can become an integral part of your daily routine. By including them in your day-to-day activities, you can strengthen your relationship and make them feel more like family. Here are some ideas on how to incorporate your cat into your everyday life:

1. **Creating a Morning Routine**

Start the Day Together:
Cats are creatures of habit, and establishing a morning routine with your cat can be a comforting ritual for both of

you. Start your day by greeting your cat with gentle strokes or a cosy lap cuddle. If your cat enjoys grooming, you might brush their fur while enjoying your morning coffee.

Shared Breakfast:
While you prepare your breakfast, feed your cat simultaneously. If your cat is a social eater, they might enjoy dining alongside you. This shared mealtime can be a bonding moment, setting a positive tone for the day ahead.

Morning Playtime:
Engage your cat in a short play session in the morning. Interactive toys, such as feather wands or laser pointers, can stimulate their natural hunting instincts and provide them with the necessary exercise to keep them healthy and active. A few minutes of play can energise your cat and help you start your day with a smile.

2. **Including Your Cat in Daily Activities**

Work From Home Companion:
If you work from home, consider creating a cosy spot for your cat near your workspace. Cats often enjoy being close to their human companions, and having them nearby can provide comfort and companionship throughout the day. A window perch or a comfy bed on your desk can make your cat feel included while allowing them to observe the world outside or nap peacefully.

Exercise Together:
While cats may not require outdoor walks like dogs, they can still participate in indoor exercise sessions. Engage your cat in interactive play, using toys that encourage jumping, chasing, or pouncing. Alternatively, invest in cat-friendly exercise equipment, such as tunnels or climbing trees, to keep them physically active.

Household Chores with Feline Assistance:
Cats are naturally curious creatures and may enjoy observing or "helping" with household chores. Encourage their participation by involving them in simple tasks, such as making the bed, folding laundry, or tidying up. While they might not be very efficient helpers, their presence can make mundane chores more enjoyable.

3. **Evening Relaxation and Wind-Down Time**

Unwind Together:
After a long day, spend some quality time unwinding with your cat. Engage in a relaxing activity, such as reading a book, watching TV, or practicing yoga. Your cat may join you on the couch or curl up beside you, providing comfort and companionship as you unwind.

Interactive Dinner Time:
Make dinnertime an interactive experience for your cat by incorporating puzzle feeders or treat-dispensing toys. These devices can engage your cat's mind and make mealtime more stimulating and enjoyable. Alternatively, use mealtime

as an opportunity to practice basic training commands, rewarding your cat with small treats for following commands like "sit" or "stay."

Bedtime Routine:
End your day with a soothing bedtime routine that includes your cat. Cats often enjoy bedtime snuggles, and allowing them to sleep nearby or on the bed can provide comfort and security. Establishing a consistent bedtime routine signals to your cat that it's time to wind down and prepare for a restful night's sleep.

Enjoying Quality Time and Creating Memorable Moments

Spending quality time with your cat is essential for building a strong bond and creating lasting memories. These moments not only strengthen your relationship but also enrich your cat's life by providing mental and emotional stimulation. Here are some ways to enjoy quality time with your feline companion:

1. **Playtime Adventures**

Interactive Play Sessions:
Interactive play is crucial for keeping your cat physically fit and mentally stimulated. Use toys that mimic prey, such as feather wands, laser pointers, or small plush toys on strings, to engage your cat's hunting instincts. Vary the toys and play activities to keep your cat interested and excited.

DIY Toys and Games:
Create DIY toys and games using household items. For example, use crumpled paper balls, cardboard boxes, or paper bags to create new play experiences. Rotate these makeshift toys regularly to maintain your cat's interest and curiosity.

Hide and Seek:
Engage your cat in a game of hide and seek by hiding behind furniture or in another room and calling their name. Encourage them to find you by making playful noises or using toys as incentives. This game taps into your cat's natural curiosity and can be a fun bonding activity.

2. **Exploration and Adventure**

Outdoor Exploration:
If your cat is comfortable with it, consider exploring the outdoors together. Use a secure harness and leash to take your cat for walks in a safe area, such as your backyard or a quiet park. Allow your cat to explore at their own pace, enjoying the sights, sounds, and smells of the outdoors.

Create an Enriched Environment:
Bring the outdoors inside by creating an enriched indoor environment. Set up bird feeders outside windows to provide your cat with entertainment, or create a window perch where they can watch the world go by. Introduce indoor plants or cat

grass for them to nibble on, ensuring all plants are safe and non-toxic to cats.

Cat-Safe Travel Adventures:
For cats comfortable with travel, consider taking them on short trips or vacations. Bring along familiar items, such as their bed or toys, to provide comfort and familiarity in new environments. Ensure your cat is safe and secure during travel, using a cat carrier or harness.

3. **Bonding Through Training and Learning**

Positive Reinforcement Training:
Training sessions can be a rewarding way to bond with your cat while teaching them useful commands or tricks. Use positive reinforcement, such as treats or praise, to encourage desired behaviours. Training not only strengthens your bond but also provides mental stimulation for your cat.

Clicker Training:
Clicker training is an effective method for teaching cats various behaviours, from basic commands to more complex tricks. Use a clicker to mark desired behaviours, followed by a treat reward. Clicker training can improve communication and understanding between you and your cat.

Problem-Solving Games:
Engage your cat in problem-solving games or puzzles to challenge their cognitive abilities. Puzzle feeders, treat-dispensing toys, or hiding treats in strategic places can

provide mental stimulation and satisfy their natural hunting instincts.

4. **Cherishing Quiet Moments**

Cozy Cuddle Sessions:
Cats often seek warmth and comfort, and cozy cuddle sessions are a perfect way to bond. Spend quiet moments cuddling with your cat on the couch or bed, providing gentle strokes or soft words of affection. These moments create a sense of security and reinforce your connection.

Quiet Companionship:
Sometimes, simply being in each other's presence is enough. Allow your cat to sit beside you while you read, work, or relax. Their quiet companionship can be calming and comforting, offering a sense of tranquility and peace.

Shared Relaxation:
Practice relaxation techniques together, such as gentle stretching or meditation. Your cat may enjoy joining you in these peaceful activities, mirroring your movements or finding a comfortable spot nearby to rest.

Embracing the Unique Quirks and Affections of Your Cat

Cats are known for their individual quirks and endearing affections. Embracing these traits and understanding what makes your cat unique can deepen your appreciation and strengthen your bond. Here's how to embrace your cat's one-of-a-kind personality:

1. **Recognising Unique Quirks**

Playful Antics:
Cats often have amusing and quirky behaviours that bring joy to their owners. Whether chasing their tail, jumping at invisible prey, or hiding in unexpected places, these antics add character and charm to your cat's personality.

Unique Vocalisations:
Some cats are naturally more vocal than others, using various sounds to communicate with their owners. Learn to recognise and respond to your cat's vocal cues, whether they're meowing for attention, chirping at birds, or purring contentedly.

Favourite Hiding Spots:
Cats love finding cozy hiding spots around the house. Embrace their preference for small spaces by providing safe and comfortable areas where they can retreat and feel secure. Respect their privacy when they choose to spend time in these hideaways.

2. **Understanding Affectionate Gestures**

Head-Butting and Purring:
Cats show affection in unique ways, such as head-butting or rubbing against you. These gestures are signs of trust and

love, marking you with their scent and claiming you as part of their territory. Purring is another common sign of contentment and affection, often accompanied by gentle kneading.

Slow Blinking:
When a cat gives you a slow blink, it's a sign of trust and affection. This behaviour is sometimes called a "kitty kiss" and can be reciprocated by slowly blinking back at your cat, reinforcing your bond.

Lap Sitting and Snuggling:
Many cats enjoy sitting on their owner's lap or snuggling beside them. This behaviour signifies comfort and trust, as they feel safe and secure in your presence. Allow your cat to initiate these snuggles, respecting their need for space when they desire it.

3. **Celebrating Individuality**

Celebrate Milestones:

Celebrate special milestones in your cat's life, such as birthdays or adoption anniversaries. Organise a small party, complete with special treats or toys, to commemorate these occasions and express your appreciation for their companionship.

Capture Memories:
Document your cat's life through photos, videos, or a dedicated journal. Capture their unique quirks, playful antics, and cherished moments to create lasting memories that you can look back on with fondness.

Respect Their Preferences:
Every cat has its likes and dislikes. Respect their preferences regarding food, play, and interaction, and adapt your approach accordingly. By acknowledging their individuality, you foster a harmonious relationship built on mutual respect and understanding.

Conclusion

Making the most of your cat's company involves incorporating them into your daily life, enjoying quality time together, and embracing their unique quirks and affections. By understanding and appreciating your cat's individuality, you can create a fulfilling and enriching relationship that enhances both your lives. Cherish the moments you share with your feline companion, and you'll find that the joys of cat ownership are as unique and rewarding as the cats themselves.

Other books from the Author:

Addu, the southernmost atoll in the Maldives, is a fascinating destination with a unique blend of natural beauty, cultural heritage and modern amenities. This enchanting atoll, also known as Seenu Atoll, is home to a vibrant community and boasts breathtaking landscapes, both above and below the water.

But this paradise is threatened by rising sea levels. According to recent studies, Addu is one of the most vulnerable atolls in the Maldives and could be completely submerged by the end of the century. Beaches threaten to erode, infrastructure is damaged and residents would have to leave their homes. The delicate marine ecosystem that supports the local economy is also at risk due to climate change.

Despite the threat, the people of Addu Atoll are resilient and determined to protect their homes. They work to raise awareness of the issue, develop sustainable practices and adapt to climate change.

ASIN : B0CTR4P65W

This story is a famous folklore in Maldives. It was originally shared as a Raivaru, a traditional song that captivated listeners with its enchanting melody and captivating narrative. Later, Mr. Abdulla Sodig immortalised this tale by transforming it into a short story. "The Stings of Dhon Kamana" was written based on the essence of that song, offering readers a deeper insight into the rich cultural heritage of the Maldives. With a casual and engaging tone, I invite you to explore the intricate tapestry of myth and mysteries woven within the narrative of this timeless folklore.

ASIN: B0CVC5DKTP

Maldives Through Time, The Ancient History of Maldives Islands" is a comprehensive exploration of the rich and fascinating history of the Maldives Islands. This book takes readers on a journey through time, from the geographical formation of the islands to the present day.

ASIN: B0CVC5DKTP

Overcome Panic Attacks
and
Live with Confidence

Overcome Panic Attacks and Live with Confidence

In "Overcoming Anxiety: A Guide to Conquering Panic Attacks," discover the essential tools and strategies to regain control of your life. This comprehensive guide delves into the root causes of anxiety and panic, offering practical advice, personal stories, and evidence-based techniques to manage and overcome these debilitating conditions. Whether you're struggling with anxiety yourself or supporting a loved one, this book provides the insight and encouragement needed to navigate the journey towards peace and confidence. Unlock the power within you to transform fear into strength and reclaim your well-being.

ISBN-13
979-8333633125

www.ingramcontent.com/pod-product-compliance
Lightning Source LLC
Chambersburg PA
CBHW070803250726
48662CB00004B/1958